Contents

What is the European Union?

The European Union (EU) is an alliance between twenty-five European countries, one of which is the UK. The EU was originally known as the European Economic Community (EEC) or 'Common Market' and then as the European Community (EC). The EU was set up to encourage trade between its members, but today its aims include co-operating in areas such as conservation, education, policing, science and finance. Some people and political parties, who were in favour of the EU's original aim of increased trade, oppose the EU's role today. They feel that it now has too much control over activities that used to be dealt with by the member countries themselves.

> 'We Europeans will always have two fatherlands. One is Europe and the other is our own country.'
> Jacques Delors, President of the EEC, 1988.

Unlike the British Parliament, where Government and Opposition sit on opposite sides of the chamber, in the European Parliament the various groups are ranged side by side in a fan shape.

Independent states

EU members are independent states, which means that each has its own elected government with powers to make its own laws. In theory, all states possess 'sovereignty' – complete control over their own affairs. In practice, the sovereignty of all states is limited by their wealth and strength and by the agreements they make with other states and international organizations through treaties.

In 2002, twelve EU members abandoned their national currencies (right) in favour of a new European currency – the Euro.

The benefits of EU membership

According to the UK Foreign and Commonwealth Office, the benefits of EU membership are as follows:

- it brings European countries closer together, thus making war between them unthinkable;
- it gives the UK access to the world's biggest single market for goods and services (455,000,000 people);
- it gives access to grants – between the years 2001 and 2006, the UK's poorer regions will benefit from EU grants totalling £10 billion;
- it creates a single European market free of tariffs and subsidies making companies compete more effectively and forcing prices down;
- it gives UK citizens the freedom to travel, study, work and live anywhere in the EU;
- it allows its members closer co-operation to tackle common problems such as pollution, crime and drug-trafficking more effectively;
- as a member of 'the most powerful club in the world', it gives the UK greater influence over the decisions made by international organizations than if it were acting alone.

Treaties The EU's powers are defined and enlarged by treaties signed by its member states. These treaties are, in effect, its constitution – the rules by which it works. The EU's founders hoped that one day it might evolve into a United States of Europe – a federation, like the USA. In a federation, the central or federal government has some powers; the rest are exercised by member states or provinces. Once a state or province joins a federation, it cannot leave it. Like the USA, Canada, Australia, India and Brazil all have federal government systems. At present the EU is more like a *con*federation, a looser system in which the states keep most of their independence, but act together for some purposes. For example, members might co-operate to share the costs of developing a new fighter plane, but decide for themselves about how and when to use it in war. In theory, member states are able to withdraw from a confederation.

The swirling shape of the European Parliament building suggests the idea that the EU is not yet complete, and will grow into something greater.

Decisions and decision-making

Decision-making in the EU is very complicated. Powers are shared between different institutions. These include:
- the European Commission (a cross between a Cabinet and a civil service, see page 16);
- the European Council (a committee of the member states' prime ministers, see page 18);
- the Council of Ministers (a committee of member states' foreign ministers, assisted by other committees of ministers, see page 18);
- the European Parliament, which is directly elected by the citizens of the twenty-five member states (page 19);
- the European Court of Justice, which interprets and enforces EU laws (page 21).

Voting The twenty-five members of the EU are very unequal in size and resources. On the most important issues, such as admitting new members to the EU, all member states of the Council of Ministers, regardless of size, must agree unanimously. A single state can therefore block major changes. On an increasingly wide range of issues, however, decisions may be made by Qualified Majority Voting (QMV), with member states' votes weighted in proportion to their population.

Member countries
This list shows when the following countries joined the EU:

1957	France, Germany, Italy, Netherlands, Belgium, Luxembourg
1973	UK, Denmark, Ireland
1981	Greece
1986	Spain, Portugal
1995	Austria, Finland, Sweden
2004	Poland, Hungary, Czech Republic, Slovakia, Slovenia, Estonia, Latvia, Lithuania, Cyprus, Malta

Regulations and directives
EU decisions take various forms:
- regulations, which must be obeyed as laws in all member states (for example, citizens of member states must be free to move to, and work in, any member country);
- directives, which are also binding but can be put into force as members think best (for example, a 1979 directive ordered that members of the European Parliament should be elected, but left it open to each country to decide how);
- decisions, which are only on bodies to which they are addressed, which may be a government, a business or even an individual (for example, a business which breaks EU rules about fair competition can be fined by the European Commission up to 10 per cent of all the money it takes in a year);
- recommendations and opinions, which are not binding.

The EU produces some 12,000 regulations, directives, decisions etc. each year.

The effect of EU membership on the UK

Laws made by EU institutions take precedence over laws made by Parliament at Westminster. In 1996, the UK government had to accept an EU decision to limit the normal working week to 48 hours. EU institutions constantly work towards 'harmonization', that is the adoption of common standards and practices throughout member states. These may be on matters ranging from the ingredients of mayonnaise to the policies individual countries should take towards immigrants, refugees and asylum-seekers. One practical example of harmonization is that all citizens of EU countries now carry the same style of passport and use the same type of driving licence.

Harmonization is limited by another important principle of EU decision-making, known as 'subsidiarity'. This means that, provided the decisions are made efficiently and accountably, they should be taken at the lowest level of government – European, national, regional or local.

The EU makes many decisions affecting everyday life in the UK. For example, foods such as fruit and vegetables must be priced in kilos and grammes, not just pounds and ounces. If goods were packaged in non-metric weights it would discriminate against consumers in countries using the metric system. This would break EU rules about selling goods freely and fairly across frontiers. Therefore the UK Parliament, civil servants in the ministries of central government and town hall officials in local government must all take account of the impact of EU decisions. Some British counties now have their own offices in Brussels, so that they can keep in close touch with EU decision-making.

In carrying the words 'European Community' and the name of the individual country, the passport carried by members of EU states reflects their dual identity.

During the 1999 elections for the European Parliament, different forms of advertising were used to urge the British people to vote. In the end, however, most didn't bother.

Divisions of opinion

UK party politics have also been deeply affected by divisions of opinion both between and within parties over relations with the EU and its powers. The Liberal Democrats and the nationalist parties in Scotland and Wales are generally enthusiastic about the EU. But within the Labour and Conservative parties there are some strongly in favour and others strongly against. Sometimes this reflects personal beliefs about UK independence, but it also indicates how the EU has affected different groups and areas. Farmers and fishermen in south-west England and factory workers in the Midlands feel that they have been hurt by EU policies. But Scotland, Wales and north-east England have benefited greatly from EU grants.

Single European currency

Most EU countries have now abolished their own separate money system in favour of a common currency, the Euro. This helps trade, finance and tourism because it is no longer necessary to change money when crossing national boundaries. Also, consumers can compare prices quoted in a single currency, no matter where a product comes from. Opponents of the Euro fear that it is the first step towards EU control of money matters generally. British 'Eurosceptics' want these matters to stay firmly in the control of the UK Parliament.

The Second World War (1939-45) cost more than fifty million lives, devastated dozens of major cities and turned millions of Europeans into stateless, homeless refugees. When the war ended, there was a clear need for a more stable international order. Even before the war's end, the governments of Belgium, the Netherlands and Luxembourg had agreed to form a closer union, called Benelux. In 1948, customs barriers were abolished between the three countries. In the same year, the Council of Europe was formed to promote co-operation between democracies. The founder members of the Council were Belgium, Denmark, France, Ireland, Italy, Luxembourg, the Netherlands, Norway, Sweden and the UK. There are now thirty-nine member countries.

Out of the ashes
In 1948, the Organization for European Economic Co-operation (OEEC) was established to share out funds from the Marshall Plan. This was a recovery scheme through which the USA gave hundreds of millions of dollars to help the nations of Western Europe repair war damage and get their peoples back to work. In 1961 the OEEC became the Organization for Economic Co-operation and Development (OECD), which promotes co-operation between the world's rich industrial nations. In 1949 the USA, Canada and the leading nations of Western Europe formed the North Atlantic Treaty Organization (NATO) to co-ordinate the defence of member states against the threat of the communist USSR and its allies.

In defeated post-war Germany, women clear bricks from a bombed-out factory for re-use.

A German poster proclaims an open highway for the Marshall Plan. United States aid was vital in rebuilding war-torn Germany.

Why unite? The main argument in favour of a more united Europe was that it would prevent war between European states, particularly France and Germany. Like NATO, it would strengthen security against the USSR. Like the Marshall Plan, it would aid the reconstruction of a shattered continent and improve economic growth. As the post-war world saw the USA and Japan emerge as global powers, it was felt that a stronger Europe was essential to preserve a distinctive cultural identity and compete against the huge US and Japanese business corporations. Finally, the states of Europe would have much greater influence in world politics if they acted together rather than alone.

First steps towards unity

Creating a more united Europe proved to be neither simple nor straightforward, and there were many delays and reverses along the way. The creation of a European Coal and Steel Community (ECSC) in 1951 co-ordinated the coal and steel industries of Germany, France, Italy and the Benelux countries. Economic co-operation between 'the Six' was further strengthened by the Treaty of Rome (1957) which set up the European Economic Community (EEC) to boost trade between members, and a European Atomic Energy Authority (Euratom) to develop the peaceful use of nuclear power.

In or out?

In 1961, the UK applied to join the EEC. As the UK's former colonies became independent, the UK needed to search elsewhere for markets for its goods. Europe began to look more attractive, particularly as the Rome treaty seemed to be helping EEC members to become richer more quickly. However, President Charles de Gaulle of France vetoed the UK's application, saying: 'Britain neither thinks nor acts like a continental nation, and so is not yet qualified for membership of the EEC.'

In 1965, France asserted its power by a boycott of EEC meetings until it was agreed that, regardless of the Rome treaty, a member state could veto any proposal it considered damaging to its vital national interests. In 1967 de Gaulle vetoed a second UK application. In the same year the ECSC, EEC and Euratom were merged into a single European Community (EC), governed by a Commission and Council of Ministers, with no internal tariffs between member states and with a common tariff against non-members. Following de Gaulle's fall from power in 1969, the UK, Denmark, Ireland and Norway were finally admitted to the EC in 1972. Norway's voters,

> **There will be boundless joy in France when Britain joins the Common Market, but there are formidable obstacles to this application.'**
> President Charles de Gaulle, 1967.

Charles de Gaulle, President of France between 1958 and 1969.

The Treaty of Rome

The treaty that established the EEC planned to bring about a common market by abolishing internal tariffs between member states, developing a common external tariff and making possible the free movement of workers, goods and money between members. The introduction to the treaty stated that those who signed it were: 'DETERMINED to lay the foundations of an ever closer union among the peoples of Europe, RESOLVED to ensure the economic and social progress of their countries by common action to eliminate the barriers which divide Europe, [and] ANXIOUS to strengthen the unity of their economies and to ensure their harmonious development by reducing the backwardness of the less favoured regions.'

however, rejected membership in a referendum. The UK confirmed its membership in 1975.

Developing common policies

In 1974, the presidents and prime ministers of member states began to meet as the European Council to develop closer co-ordination of national policies on global issues. In 1975, the Lomé Agreement was signed. This agreed to organize EC aid to forty-six developing countries in Africa, the Pacific and the Caribbean, many of them former colonies of EC members. It was a first step towards a common foreign policy.

Signing the Treaty of Rome in 1957. This laid the foundations for the European Economic Community (EEC).

Direct elections At first members of the European Parliament were nominated by member states but since 1979 they have been directly elected by citizens. In Belgium, Greece and Portugal voting is compulsory so the turnout is high. In 2004 the average turnout across the EU was 45%, but only 38% of the electorate voted in the UK and just 21% voted in Poland.

Enlargement In 1979 a European Monetary System (EMS) was created to prevent the value of different European currencies varying too much from one another. This was a first step towards creating a single European currency, common to all member states. Enthusiasts not only wanted to 'broaden' the EC by adding new members but also to 'deepen' it by increasing its powers and range of concerns. The Single European Act (1985) formalized the unofficial

UK attitudes
One reason for the UK's lack of enthusiasm towards the EU may simply be the strength of UK links with the rest of the English-speaking world, through trade, migration and the shared heritage of a common culture, laws and institutions. Many British families have relatives in North America, Australia and the Caribbean. There are also strong business, entertainment and sporting links with these areas. A further reason could be the hostility of a number of popular UK newspapers towards the EU, which they tend to show as wasteful, irrelevant, interfering or simply corrupt.

A Survey of British attitudes in 2004

EU membership has been: Good 36%, Bad 33%, Neither 22%, Don't Know 9%

The EU should have: More Powers 14%, Less 55%, Same 18%, Don't Know 13%

Britain should: Stay in the EU 60%, Withdraw 28%, Don't Know 12%

Euro coinage (above) and notes went into circulation in January 2002. The Euro coin has a map of Europe on one side, and a differing national design on the other.

meetings of heads of government that took place at the end of each state's six-month presidency and created a formal body for the purpose, the European Council. It also modified the Rome treaty to introduce QMV on all matters related to the creation of a 'single market'. This meant going beyond the removal of tariff barriers to the removal, by 1992, of all other barriers, such as work permits.

At Maastricht: John Major (left), UK Prime Minister from 1990-97, with Helmut Kohl, the German Chancellor who reunited West and East Germany in 1990.

In 1992 a Treaty on European Union, signed at Maastricht in the Netherlands, amended the Single European Act in favour of even closer co-operation on political, defence, environmental, legal and economic matters. The Maastricht Treaty included a Social Chapter, which set out basic welfare rights and the creation of a European Monetary Union (EMU) with a single currency. The process of membership enlargement, however, made reaching agreements increasingly difficult.

The 1997 Treaty of Amsterdam extended the system of QMV to decisions made by the Council of Ministers. It also set out common rules on citizenship and immigration. Applications for membership from twelve more countries made it necessary to revise the way EU institutions worked yet again. In particular, the over-weighting of votes in favour of smaller countries was adjusted. In 2001, the Treaty of Nice rearranged the weighting system in favour of larger countries, like the UK.

'To try and suppress nationhood and concentrate power at the centre of a European conglomerate would be highly damaging. Europe will be stronger precisely because it has France as France, Spain as Spain, Britain as Britain, each with its own customs, traditions and identity...' In a speech given at Bruges in Belgium in 1988, the British Prime Minister Margaret Thatcher warned against further progress towards political unity. Her 'Eurosceptic' approach is still supported by some Members of Parliament and sectors of the UK popular press.

Most states have a legislature (parliament) to make laws, an executive (government) to enforce them and a judiciary (court system) to decide how they should be applied. The EU is different because the legislative and executive powers are shared between the European Commission, the Council of Ministers and the European Parliament.

The European Commission The

Commission puts forward suggestions for new regulations and directives, draws up the budget for the EU as a whole and ensures that EU decisions are upheld and applied by member states. The Commission's most important task is to set the EU's agenda, in other words to suggest what it should do next. In this sense, it is like the Cabinet of a national government. While a Cabinet is headed by a prime minister, the Commission is headed by a president appointed by the European Council and approved by the European Parliament. The president has less power than a prime minister because he or she can neither appoint nor dismiss the other commissioners nor decide which job each should do.

Powerhouse of policy-making – the European Commission building in Brussels, Belgium.

The Commission is also the EU's civil service, carrying out EU programmes. Because the Commission deals with many international bodies (such as the World Trade Organization) on behalf of member states, it is also the EU's diplomatic service. Any agreements negotiated by the Commission, however, must get final approval from the Council of Ministers.

The Commission has a central staff of over 20,000. One third of all Commission employees are translators or interpreters, coping with the need to make information available in each of the Community's twenty languages. Twenty-five commissioners, appointed for five years, supervise the work of the Commission. Each one has responsibility for different areas of EU activity. These may be a single field such as transport or agriculture, or may be quite mixed areas, for example Energy, Tourism and Small Businesses or Consumer Affairs, Fisheries and Humanitarian Aid. Most commissioners are former politicians, though they may be businessmen or trade union leaders. In 2004 it was proposed that the number of commissioners should be cut to 17 with effect from 2014.

A Commission meeting plans a special summit to choose a new president for the EC.

Overseeing its work

The Commission is overseen by the European Parliament, which has powers to examine its working. The Parliament's most important power is that it can dismiss the commissioners – but they must all be dismissed at the same time! The Commission is assisted in its work by a dozen agencies which, unlike the central EU institutions, are deliberately distributed among different member states. The European Environment Agency is located in Copenhagen, Denmark, the Agency for Health and Safety at Work in Bilbao, Spain, and so on.

The European Council

When heads of EU governments meet together three or four times a year to consider major issues they do so as the European Council. The Council considers the most basic questions, such as the powers of the EU institutions, EU membership and methods of working and decision-making. Monthly meetings of member states' foreign ministers (known as the General Affairs Council of the Council of Ministers) deal with routine matters. These meetings are chaired by the foreign minister of whichever member state currently holds the presidency of the Council of Ministers. When specific, rather than general issues are being discussed, such as a change in taxation

In 1999, a number of EU commissioners were accused of corruption and, as a result, all the commissioners resigned. Former UK Labour Party leader, Neil Kinnock (bottom row, far left), one of the replacement team of commissioners, was ordered to reform Commission work methods to prevent future abuses of budgets, expenses and appointments.

or a road project, then specialist finance ministers, transport ministers etc. will attend or may meet separately. As all these meetings take place at intervals, a Committee of Permanent Representatives (COREPER) ensures the smooth running of affairs by meeting weekly. COREPER is made up of ambassadors from the member states of the EU. Unlike in a nation state, where legislation is made by a parliament, in the EU laws are proposed by the Commission and adopted by the Council. The opinion of the European Parliament must be taken but need not be followed.

European finance ministers pose for the press after a signing ceremony in 1998. This event marked the point at which those countries that signed were locked together in the Euro.

The European Parliament

The Parliament's 732 MEPs are elected for a term of five years. Unlike national elections, however, European elections do not change the EU's government, which is the European Commission and Council of Ministers, or the programme of proposals that the Commission intends to have passed into law.

The range of parties represented in the European Parliament is often different from those represented in national parliaments. 'Greens', who put environmental issues at the top of their list, are much more strongly represented at the European level than in most national parliaments. The European Parliament contains twelve members of the UK Independence Party (whose main aim is to get the UK to withdraw altogether from the EU). There are also anti-EU MEPs from France, Poland and Sweden.

Split-site Parliament
The effective working of the European Parliament is hampered by the fact that activities are split between three sites. Full meetings take place in Strasbourg, committees meet in Brussels and the secretariat (which takes care of its paperwork in eleven languages) is based in Luxembourg. Most MEPs believe that they would work much more effectively if everything was concentrated in Brussels, so that they could be close to the other main EU institutions. However, France and Luxembourg are strongly opposed to such a change, which can only be made with unanimous agreement.

Blocs MEPs do not sit and vote together as national groupings but as party 'blocs'. The largest of these are the European People's Party-European Democrats (which has 268 members, including UK Conservatives) and the Socialists (which has 200 members, including UK Labour). Voting in the European Parliament is less predictable than in national parliaments and on some issues MEPs may form temporary alliances outside their usual party blocs.

In its early days the European Parliament was dismissed as a powerless 'talking shop'. Its democratic standing was greatly raised by the introduction of direct elections in 1979; before then its members were appointed by governments, which made it more of an advisory panel than a true parliament. Since then, voters in every member country have voted directly for their MEPs. The Parliament has powers to:

- question both the Commission and the Council;
- amend or reject the EU budget;
- dismiss the entire Commission.

It also must give final approval for new members applying to join the EU. The Maastricht Treaty gave the European Parliament a new right to require the Commission to propose action on a particular problem that the Parliament feels is being overlooked.

The EU has been criticized for having a glaring gap between its institutions and the citizens they are supposed to serve. Many European citizens are only vaguely aware of how it is organized, how it

The European Investment Bank This bank, founded in 1958 and based in Luxembourg, makes loans to finance major projects, such as improving communications, both in the poorer regions of the EU and as part of the EU's aid programme to developing countries. It also supports the London-based European Bank for Reconstruction and Development, set up in 1991 to make loans to the new democracies of Eastern Europe, such as Hungary and Poland.

Dual identity – the 'E' on this Christmas stamp shows the uniform charge for posting to EU countries. The Queen's profile shows that the stamp is British.

works, how it affects them and how they can affect it. If the EU is to close that gap, many see increasing interest in the European Parliament and trust in its authority as the best way forward.

The European Court of Justice (ECJ)

The ECJ sits in Luxembourg and exists to interpret EU law and ensure that it is enforced. It deals with six types of cases:

- Disputes between the EU itself and member states. These are the most common, and usually involve cases brought by the Commission against a country that has failed to implement laws as required by treaty.
- Disputes between member states.
- Disputes between the institutions of the EU itself, for example, over their respective powers.
- Disputes between the EU and individuals or corporate bodies.
- Giving opinions on the legal aspects of international agreements.
- Giving preliminary rulings on cases referred to it by national courts. This is extremely important because it ensures that EU law is applied uniformly throughout member states.

Belgian soccer player Jean-Marc Bosman, centre, flanked by his lawyers at the European Court of Justice in Luxembourg, September 1995. Bosman claimed that his career was ruined by his team FC Liège's failure to honour a transfer agreement for him to move to French club Dunkerke.

How the ECJ works

The Court is made up of twenty-five judges (one from each member state) and eight advocates-general appointed, by the Council of Ministers, for six years. The advocates-general assist the judges by examining the arguments submitted by the two parties in dispute and proposing a solution.

The decisions of the ECJ may overrule national law and are binding. There is no higher court of appeal. ECJ procedures differ from those of UK courts in the following respects:

- the ECJ's judgments are given as though they were unanimous;
- only the judges themselves and their officials know who voted which way to reach their decision;
- decision-making is usually a two-stage process in which advocates-general give a provisional opinion, which is usually endorsed by the judges, but may be ignored.

The ECJ has no direct powers to enforce its judgments and relies on member states to do so, but it has never been defied. Its judgments are most notable in the field of commerce, which is interpreted very broadly. For example, the Court ruled that football clubs could not be ordered to limit the number of foreign players in their teams because that would limit the free movement of labour between EU member states. Court rulings also affect such matters as social security, as it has ruled in favour of equal pay and pension rights for men and women.

Court of Auditors

This body is not a court in the sense that the ECJ is. It is the task of the Court of Auditors to check that EU funds have been spent correctly, which means both legally and efficiently. Its annual reports have exposed many cases of waste, especially in agricultural payments, as well as cases of outright fraud. The Court's report on the EU's 1997 budget found that at least £3 billion had been mis-spent. Examples include paying grants to fishermen to improve safety standards on boats that had already sunk, and payment of subsidies to farmers who exaggerated the area of land they farmed by up to 20 per cent.

The European Court of Justice in Luxembourg. Important cases are tried by all the judges sitting as a single body.

The European Court of Human Rights (ECHR)

This is a separate body, sitting in Strasbourg, established by the Council of Europe to enforce the 1950 European Convention for the Protection of Human Rights and Fundamental Freedoms. The original convention established very basic rights such as banning torture, forced labour and discrimination and guaranteeing the right to a fair trial and freedom of religion. Further protocols have been added to cover additional rights such as education and free elections. Over the years, the ECHR has given rulings on the freedom of the press, on corporal punishment in schools and on the rights of suspected terrorists. The ECHR is not part of the machinery of the European Union, but EU member states are expected to have signed up to the European Convention, although the EU itself has not. Currently, forty-five states have agreed to accept the rulings of the ECHR. Acceptance into the Council of Europe is usually seen as a first step towards acceptance into the EU itself.

Mrs Diane Blood (above) announces the birth of her son at a press conference in December 1998. The ECHR upheld her legal right to use the sperm of her dead husband to have a child.

The European Court of Human Rights building in Strasbourg was designed by British architect, Richard Rogers.

The average citizen pays about fifty times as much per year in taxes to his or her national government as to the EU. The main source of EU revenue is a share (just over one per cent) of the Value Added Tax collected in each country.

More than 40 per cent of EU spending goes towards the Common Agricultural Policy (CAP). This was introduced in 1962 to guarantee European farmers' incomes against undercutting by food imports from cheaper non-EU producers. In practice, the CAP enabled some farmers to go on being inefficient because they knew that they would receive the same incomes anyway. CAP payments were soon gobbling up three-quarters of the entire EU budget. Although a fall in the number of European farmers has cut this percentage drastically, the CAP still encourages the production of more crops than are needed and leads to a situation in which farmers are paid not to grow things. The need for further reform is widely acknowledged.

Other major items of EU spending are:
- regional policy – this helps regions that are either traditionally poor (for example, many parts of southern Italy) or have been hit by industrial decline (for example, Northern Ireland);
- social policy – this pays for skills training programmes to cut unemployment, especially among the young, the disabled, women and migrant workers;
- development co-operation – this provides emergency food aid to disaster areas and invests in long-term projects to overcome poverty in more than 70 developing countries. Other budgets are devoted to energy-saving

The Common Agricultural Policy has been criticized for creating crop surpluses which have had to be destroyed or expensively stored.

projects, scientific and industrial research, transport improvements and environmental conservation.

Some EU achievements

The EU is now the world's biggest trading unit. Since 1993 it has been a single market for the free movement of labour, goods and money. The EU has also developed common standards for trademarks, patents, packaging, labelling and the safety of medicines, foodstuffs, toys and machinery. The adoption of the Euro as a common currency is seen by many as the logical next step for making the single market work even better.

In the field of technology, EU funding has enabled EU countries to compete with leading US plane-makers by enabling them to co-operate to build the European Airbus, a plane that no single country could have afforded to develop alone. The EU has also funded hundreds of projects to encourage closer co-operation between businesses and universities in such fields as telecommunications, information technology, new materials technology and biotechnology. The Apollo project, for example, developed satellites for transmitting extremely large amounts of information.

Apart from abolishing customs duties, the single European market has also brought about the dismantling of some three hundred 'non-tariff barriers'. One such was the refusal to recognize another country's educational or professional qualifications. Now, thanks to the EU, the qualifications of professional people, such as doctors and architects, are recognized in a range of European countries.

Where transport is concerned, in the interests of road safety the EU has enforced the fitting of tachographs in heavy goods vehicles. These devices record how fast and for how many hours the vehicle has been travelling, and can be used to enforce speed limits and regular rest periods for drivers so that they do not become over-tired.

The EU has also developed environmental programmes including the banning of leaded petrol, campaigns against seal hunting and 'naming and shaming' seaside resorts with dirty bathing beaches. Consumer protection programmes have involved detailed health and safety regulations governing the use of colourings and preservatives in foodstuffs. They have also ensured that products such as honey, fruit juice, jams and diet foods measure up to acceptable standards of purity. The EU has advanced women's rights by upholding equal treatment in matters such as pay, pensions and promotion and securing special rights such as maternity leave. Education programmes have encouraged students to study abroad, developed better language teaching methods and helped to preserve minority languages, such as Gaelic.

In the cultural field the EU has used scholarships, prizes, grants and festivals to support young artists and performers. The EU funds an annual European Film Festival and designates a European City of Culture each year, where EU funds pay for arts events and exhibitions. It has also funded the conservation of such major European landmarks as the Parthenon in Athens, the Doge's Palace in Venice and the Alhambra Palace at Granada.

The Parthenon in Athens, Greece, is a symbol of the cultural heritage of the ancient world that is shared by all Europeans.

European leaders keep saying that the future of the EU depends on what European citizens want it to be – but that depends on citizens being interested enough in the EU to want to have a say. Interest in and support for the EU varies between countries and has also varied over time. Support varies too within national populations, tending to be stronger among the young, the better educated and the better off.

Possible Europes

The possibilities for a future Europe may be very different from what the original signatories of the Treaty of Rome imagined. The Nice treaty's acceptance that groups of states might co-operate more closely on particular matters within the EU framework without involving every other member state has opened up the possibility of what has been called a 'two-speed' or 'variable geometry' Europe. This means that some states, such as the Benelux countries or the states around the Baltic (for example, Estonia or Lithuania), might choose to merge their transport systems or welfare services or armed forces, while more 'Eurosceptic' nations, such as the UK, or newcomers too poor as yet to join in, held off.

'The...member states of the EU are far more diverse than the original thirteen colonies [which became the United States of America].... Apart from language and cultural differences they are all sovereign states, several of them with hundreds of years of Independence behind them.... It is reasonable to expect that some form of federal government for Western Europe may eventually emerge.... It is unrealistic... that it would have powers as extensive as those in the USA or that France, Italy and Spain should find themselves on a level with Ohio, Pennsylvania or Kansas.'
Dick Leonard, a former British MP.

EU funding has helped to build the Channel Tunnel (above), new airports in Greece and Italy and the M6 extension and Manchester Metrolink in the UK.

What next? A two-level Europe has already emerged over the Euro. Swedish voters turned it down in 2003, while Estonia, Lithuania and Slovenia pledged to join by 2007. The new members from Eastern Europe have a long way to go in terms of catching up with the wealth of other EU countries. In 2004 the annual wealth produced by all ten new members combined was just 5% of the wealth produced by the existing fifteen members.

The application of Romania (pictured above) to join the EU may be delayed, not only due to its poverty but because of its corruption and lack of independent judges and a free press.

A Constitution for Europe

In 2004 EU member states agreed a new constitution, but a number of EU countries still have to confirm their agreement to the constitution in a referendum.

Major changes in the constitution include:

1. European Parliament powers to block laws to be increased.

2. Greater EU powers over justice, asylum and immigration policy.

3. A Qualified Majority Vote will require a minimum of 15 states representing 65% of the population.

4. The rotating presidency will be replaced by a president chosen by member states and confirmed by the European Parliament.

5. An EU Foreign Minister and diplomatic service should be established.

6. The right of members to withdraw will be recognised.

Whatever the shortcomings of the EU more states still want to join it. Bulgaria, Romania and Croatia aim to join by 2007. Turkey has been trying to join since 1963; it has improved its human rights record but it is still not wealthy enough, with only a quarter of the wealth of the average EU country. As Turkey has more people than all ten newcomers of 2004 put together, its impact on the EU budget would be great. Other possible applicants include former parts of the Soviet Union such as the Ukraine, Belarus, Armenia, Azerbaijan, Georgia and Moldova; and Mediterranean states like Morocco and Tunisia which are former European colonies.

Schoolchildren watching the work of the European Parliament on a 'Euroschool' day.

Activity
1. Choose a European city and visit its web site to find out which other European cities it has links with and how these work.
2. Write the words for a new anthem for the European Union.
3. You have been put in charge of arranging a ten-day study tour of the European Union for a group of visiting students from North America. What would you show them? Who would you want them to meet? What would you want them to experience? Draw up a day-by-day schedule for the group. Say how you would follow up the tour and how you could judge whether it had been a success.

Glossary

accession the act of signing up to an agreement or joining an institution

accountability being held responsible for one's actions

advocate-general the title given to officials of the European Court of Justice who give preliminary rulings

asylum seekers people looking for a safe country to live in

biotechnology the science of changing or manipulating living things

boycott to have absolutely nothing to do with

Cabinet the most important decision-making body in a government

Christian Democrats a type of moderate, conservative political party found in several Catholic countries of Europe

civil servant a person employed by government to carry out its policies

colony a country which is not independent but ruled by another country

commerce buying and selling goods or services

common tariff a tariff shared by two or more countries

communism a system of government in which all business is under the control of a single political party, in theory for the benefit of all

conglomerate an organization consisting of several units but managed as a single system

conservation taking care of the environment

corporal punishment beating

cultural identity the beliefs, customs, traditions and symbols which make a nation, community or ethnic group different from others

customs barriers limits on the free trade of goods or services created by imposing a tariff, quota (limited amount) or regulation (such as a health or safety standard)

customs duties money raised from the payment of tariffs

democracies countries with governments chosen by free and fair elections

designate to choose or appoint

direct elections elections in which voters themselves choose their representatives, such as Members of Parliament or local councillors, rather than having them appointed by others

directives written instructions having the force of law

Eurosceptic a person who believes that the further development or strengthening of the European Union is unwise or impractical

foreign minister a member of a government who is chiefly responsible for its dealings with international bodies and foreign countries

Gaelic the original language of Ireland and parts of Scotland

grant a sum of money given for spending for a particular purpose

immigrants people who have come to settle in a country

inefficient not working as well as it should

internal tariff a tariff imposed inside a country

international order the framework of treaties, institutions and customs which controls dealings between international organizations and countries

migrant workers people who have to leave home to find work

migration the movement of people, for example, from one country to another

ministry a department of government in charge of a particular activity, such as defence, education or health

nation state an independent country whose people share a common identity and rights as citizens

national parliament a country's most important elected law-making body

new materials technology a field of knowledge relating to the use of hi-tech, man-made materials such as carbon fibres

patent a legal document giving an inventor the right to stop other people from copying his or her invention

preliminary ruling a legal decision which may be changed as a result of a challenge on a point of law or fact, or an appeal to a higher court

protocol a document setting out points of agreement in detail

purity standards regulations to make sure that goods such as foodstuffs or medicines are free from decay or contamination

Qualified Majority Voting a system of decision-making used by the European Union to avoid making all decisions unanimous. Member countries are given votes roughly according to their size.

referendum a poll giving voters the chance to decide on a single issue

refugees people leaving a country on account of ill treatment, war or disaster

regulations written rules with the force of law

signatory a person, body or country who has signed up to an agreement

single market a trading area with no internal tariffs

social security a system of welfare payments for the old, sick, disabled and unemployed

socialist a member of a political party which is committed to using government powers to make people more equal

subsidy a grant from taxes to support an industry or activity

superstate a country made up of and controlling several states

tariff a tax on goods imported (brought in) from abroad

treaty a written, legal agreement between countries or international organizations

unanimous all agreeing together, without exception

USSR the Union of Soviet Socialist Republics, a communist superstate dominated by Russia, which lasted from 1922 to 1991

Value Added Tax a tax charged on a product or service at each stage of its creation

veto to ban

Resources

Information books

You may find the following books useful:

The European Union (seventh edition), Ali El-Agraa, Pearson Education, 2004

A Geography of the European Union, John Cole and Francis Cole, Routledge, 1997

The State of the European Union: Risks, Reforms, Renewals and Revival, Maria Green Cowles, Oxford University Press, 2001

Encyclopaedia of the European Union, Desmond Dinan, Palgrave, 2000

Understanding the European Union: A Concise Introduction, John McCormick, Palgrave, 2002

The Building of the European Union (third edition), John Pinder, Oxford Paperbacks, 1998

Policy-Making in the European Union, Helen Wallace and William Wallace, Oxford University Press, 2000

Understanding European Union Institutions, Alex Warleigh, Routledge, 2001

The internet

The best site for general reference is the BBC site (**http://www.bbc.co.uk**) and those of national newspapers, including:

http://www.guardian.co.uk and
http://www.dailytelegraph.co.uk

Index

Numbers in **bold** refer to illustrations.